8.99

A Practical Guide to the Computer Misuse Act 1990

Tony Elbra

L

NCC Blackwell

MANCHESTER • OXFORD

British Library Cataloguing In Publication Data

A Practical Guide to the Computer Misuse Act 1990

1. Great Britain. Computer systems. Law

1. National Computing Centre

344.1064

ISBN 1-85554-077-0

First published in 1990 by:

NCC Blackwell Limited, 108 Cowley Road, Oxford OX4 1JF, England

Editorial Office: The National Computing Centre Limited, Oxford House, Oxford Road, Manchester M1 7ED, England.

Typeset in 11pt Bembo by ScribeTech Ltd, Bradford, West Yorkshire; and printed by Hobbs the Printers of Southampton.

ISBN 1-85554-077-0

Acknowledgements

The author acknowledges the assistance given by John Head-Rapson
of the Department of Trade and Industry and by Chris Hook of the
NCC in the preparation of this book.

Foreword

It is a truism that there are too many lawyers in Parliament with a vested interest in producing unintelligible legislation for which they can then charge exorbitant fees for interpretation to the layman.

I am glad to say that I am no lawyer and the Computer Misuse Act 1990 which I steered through Parliament is as intelligible as I can make it. Having said that, I must confess that, as we simplified the general provision in the Bill during its passage, the clauses on jurisdiction became necessarily more complicated.

I am therefore delighted to welcome this booklet, written by Tony Elbra of the National Computing Centre Ltd, which advises you how you may best make use of this new legislation.

When I drew Number Three in the ballot for Private Members Bills, I was deluged with helpful suggestions for legislation, but it was not until the Aids Diskette scandal hit the headlines, that I looked seriously at computer crime.

This matter is so serious that we had hoped for a Government Bill, but the Law Commission Study on the subject of computer crime laws was published in October 1989, by which time the Queen's Speech containing the Government's legislative programme for that Session of Parliament was finalised.

To have delayed legislating until 1990/91 could have cost Britain billions of pounds of damage to computer systems, so here was a measure which was urgently required and had general appeal, because computers affect the everyday lives of all of us.

The Act provides a coherent regime for the prosecution of those who misuse computers. It has been framed specifically to deal with the new mischiefs which modern technology has brought. The police now have the power to prosecute computer misuse without the need, in some cases, to try and stretch the existing criminal law. The Act gives a clear signal to future generations of would-be hackers that computer misuse will no longer be tolerated by society.

The Act can, however, only complement and not replace, security procedures. Prevention is, after all, better than cure. Users will have to examine their existing security procedures and possibly re-define the authority of users on their systems if they are to receive the full support of the law.

My message to computer users is that Parliament has done its bit – now it is up to you to do yours.

MICHAEL COLVIN
Member of Parliament for Romsey and Waterside

Contents

Introduction

On 29 June 1990 the Computer Misuse Act received the Royal Assent and became law. The Act came into operation on 29 August 1990 and, from that date, it became a criminal offence for anyone to access or modify computer-held data or software without authority or to attempt to do so.

The Act creates three specific offences to deal with the problems of hacking, viruses and other nuisances which have plagued computer users for such a long time. It obviates the previously existing need, when miscreants of this sort were detected, of trying to fit laws intended for other purposes to computer misuse. These have, in the past, included charges of criminal damage, forgery, telecommunications misuse or even abstraction of electricity, with varying degrees of success.

The Computer Misuse Act will be subject to interpretation by the courts. There will be no specially appointed supervisory body with respect to this Act as there is with the Data Protection Act. Therefore, the true extent of the Act will only appear as case law builds up and as various prosecutions achieve success or failure.

This book is intended to explain the Act as it is perceived immediately after Royal Assent. It cannot take into account future interpretations. It is hoped that the book will be of help to computer users in explaining the implications of the offences created.

Neither is this book intended to be a definitive and legally-based dissertation on the Computer Misuse Act. It is intended only as a practical guide for computer users. Some parts of the Act are ignored altogether where these seem of more interest to the lawyer than the computer user. Sections of the Act are quoted, however, for those that wish to follow up any reference.

The Computer Misuse Act 1990 is available from Her Majesty's Stationery Office at a charge (in 1990) of £2.90.

1   Purpose of the Act

Computer misuse has been the subject of detailed study and debate over the last five years or so. The two main studies were carried out by the Scottish Law Commission (1987) and the Law Commission for England and Wales (1989) [both in Appendix A].

These studies identified a number of different types of misuse, some of which were considered to be already covered. However, both Law Commissions considered that certain types of computer misuse now merited the sanctions of the *criminal* law. The English Law Commission, as a result of more comprehensive and up to date information, went further than its Scottish counterpart and proposed new criminal offences for simple unauthorised access and for unauthorised modification of the contents of computers. They also suggested an aggravated 'hacking' offence similar to that proposed by the Scottish Law Commission in 1987. In particular, they proposed a two–tier structure of offences – simple 'hacking' and 'hacking in pursuit of a further serious crime'.

The English Law Commission concluded that 'hacking' or unauthorised access was sufficiently widespread to be a matter of major and legitimate concern to computer users. This was because of the actual losses and costs incurred by computer system owners whose systems had been breached; the fact that unauthorised entry might be a preliminary to more serious offences; and that confidence in computer systems was being undermined. They also observed that an unauthorised modification offence had the full support of those who responded to their consultative paper; it amounted to electronic sabotage or damage.

In suggesting the offences and their broad terms, the Commission suggested the rationale for them was that the conduct they sought to deter threatened the integrity of computers and undermined the trust held in them by their owners. The Commisssion found that increasing reliance was being placed on computers, not simply for information storage but more for operational purposes. They highlighted the fact that the correct functioning of certain systems could be a matter of life and death and the potential for mischief in some circumstances very great. This rationale was accepted by the sponsor of the Bill (Michael Colvin, the Member of Parliament for Romsey and Waterside), the Government and the legislature.

Recognition of the underlying purpose is important in gaining an understanding of the Terms and the implications of the Computer Misuse Act 1990 which are set out in the following chapters.

2 Description of the Offences

USERS' RESPONSIBILITIES

The Computer Misuse Act places no additional burdens on bona fide computer users, but introduces powers to prosecute those that deliberately and without authorisation, misuse computer systems belonging to their employers or to third parties. Unlike the Data Protection Act, this piece of legislation is not restricted to any particular type of data or application and there is no Registrar or other supervisory body to enforce it. Computer users should ensure that they themselves and their employees uphold the principles of the Computer Misuse Act.

Whilst the Computer Misuse Act will satisfy many computer users who have been clamouring for an anti-hacking law, and will deter at least some hackers, it will not help the users to prevent or detect anyone misusing their computer systems. However, where by their own devices they are able to identify a hacker, potential fraudster or unauthorised modifier, the Act will give a basis for prosecution.

ENFORCEMENT

As with most criminal offences, enforcement is the responsibility of the police. If the Act is to succeed it is most important that prosecutions should be brought, otherwise the Act may come to be regarded as a 'dead letter' and its deterrent effect will be lost. It is equally important that prosecutions should be successful; if not, the law will be treated with contempt.

3

THE OFFENCES

The Act defines three offences. These are: unauthorised access to computer programs or data, unauthorised access with a further criminal intent ('ulterior intent'), and unauthorised modification of computer material, that is programs and data for the time being held in the computer.

2.1   The Unauthorised Access Offence

Whilst the offence was created, in part, to deter the practice of 'hacking' (whereby a person outside an organisation would deliberately set out to explore a system which he knew well he was not authorised to access), authorised users who decide to exceed their authority to access parts of the system officially denied to them are equally as guilty, and are more prevalent. It is estimated that 70% – 80% of unauthorised access is carried out by 'insiders'.

The legislators, acting on the advice of the Law Commission, therefore wished the definition of the offence to extend to all persons that accessed the data or software without authority.

Section 1(1) of the Act reads thus:

A person is guilty of an offence if—

(a) he causes a computer to perform any function with intent to secure access to any program or data held in any computer;

(b) the access he intends to secure is un-authorised; and

(c) he knows at the time that he causes the function that that is the case.

Therefore, to prove the offence it will be necessary to show: that the access was deliberate; that it was unauthorised; and that the alleged miscreant knew it was unauthorised.

Section 1(2) removes many possible excuses from the offender.

The intent a person has to have to commit an offence under this Section need not be directed at –

(a)   any particular program or data;

(b)   a program or data of any particular kind; or

(c)   a program or data held in any particular computer.

A person accused of an offence under this Section alone would be tried in a Magistrates' or Sheriff's Court. He faces a fine of up to £2000 or imprisonment for up to six months (the most such courts can impose), or both these punishments. Both these penalties are twice what the Law Commission suggested. The Commission recommended that imprisonment should only be used in cases of the most deliberate and persistent misuse of this sort.

Unauthorised access will cover both those seeking access from outside who will, in most cases, be unable to demonstrate any consent, and authorised users that deliberately exceed their authority. The offence lies in 'causing the computer in question to perform any function with the deliberate intent to secure access to programs and data held in the computer and in the knowledge that this is unauthorised'. This has the effect of excluding any purely physical approach to the hardware from the offence; it also means that anyone who carries out passive eavesdropping (either physically or electronically) by overlooking a screen or printout is excluded, as an eavesdropper cannot cause the computer deliberately to perform any extra function.

An offender who successfully obtains access and makes the computer display data or listings of a program will plainly be in contravention of the Act. Others who are less successful may also commit the offence. For example, if the offender was trying out guessed passwords, he would be guilty the moment any computer responded with a message stating that the password used was invalid. He would be guilty even before that time, if, as a result of his action, the computer invited him to provide a password, as that invitation would constitute a computer function carried out as a result of the offender's actions.

A hacker who, with intent to secure unauthorised access, goes into the telephone network to find out if any computers will respond will be guilty the moment one of them does. It is immaterial whether it was the one which he expected to respond or if he has any idea which computer it is.

An authorised user who deliberately exceeds his carefully prescribed authority in order to look at data or software from which he was normally excluded would be as guilty of this offence as a hacker from outside the organisation; for example, a member of the accounts department who broke into records intended for exclusive personnel use would commit the offence, even though, in his own field, he has authority to access the organisation's data. A further example is where facilities are provided for a client to look at only his own account, anyone who intentionally looked at someone else's account would be guilty.

However, the offence is deliberately phrased to exclude anybody genuinely blundering into a system or network without authority. So, someone who dials the wrong number in error or who enters an anagram of their password with unexpected results would not be treated as being in breach of the Act. The offender must have the intention of accessing and know that he has no authority to do so. However, he does not need to intend to access any particular computer; he may cause one computer to function as a means of checking his identity in his search for another.

The other offences are regarded as much more serious and accordingly attract much higher penalties.

2.2   The Ulterior Intent Offence

The Act views matters more gravely if the unauthorised access, instead of being just a means of unorthodox amusement or exploration, is used to further some more serious crime.

Hence, Section 2(1):

A person is guilty of an offence under this Section if he commits ..the 'unauthorised access offence' (see

2.1 above) with intent –

(a) to commit an offence...; or

(b) to facilitate the commission of...an offence (whether by himself or by some other person).

In order for the ulterior intent offence to be proved, it will be necessary to show: that the accused deliberately accessed a computer; that he did not have authority to do so; that he knew he was unauthorised; and that he had the intention of using the information gained (either at the time or later) to commit some further offence.

Offences of this sort attract a maximum sentence of five years imprisonment and/or an unlimited fine. This penalty is a ten-fold increase on that recommended for simple hacking, and indicates the greatly increased seriousness of the offence. However, it would plainly be unfair to impose a five year sentence if the intended further offence was of a minor nature, for example using the computer to evade parking charges. The Act makes it clear that Section 2 would only apply if the further intended offence itself carried a maximum sentence of five years or more.

The offence involves unauthorised access to a computer system with the intention to carry out or facilitate the commission of a further serious crime. For example, access could be made to a number of computers in preparation for a computer fraud or access could be made to personal information as a step towards attempting blackmail.

Though fraud and blackmail are offences already and even attempting to commit them is also an offence, this new offence was thought necessary. Under normal circumstances a person cannot be charged with an attempted offence unless what has been done is more than merely preparatory to the commission of the offence. However, when computers are involved, once the preparatory stages are over the offence can be put into operation with lightning speed. It is then too late to prevent the consequences, which, in the case of fraud, can be very expensive. The ulterior intent offence will mean that persons can be charged as soon as they use a computer with a provable intent to carry out a more serious crime, without the need to wait until their plans are further advanced.

Section 2 goes on to remove some of the excuses that a person accused of this offence might offer. It is immaterial whether the further offence (fraud or blackmail, for example) is to be committed at the same time as the unauthorised access or at a later date. Nor does it matter if the subsequent offence is to be carried out on the same computer, another computer or no computer at all. Neither does it matter if the further offence is in fact impossible. The important factor is the intention to commit it. When, how and the likelihood of success are irrelevant.

Cases brought under Section 2 may be tried in either type of court (Magistrates' Court or Crown Court, Sheriff's Court or High Court). The lower courts will be restricted in the sentence that they pass but may, if necessary, refer anyone found guilty to a higher court for a sentence beyond their powers. Someone found not guilty of the ulterior intent offence may still be found guilty of simple hacking, the unauthorised access offence. This may occur even if the case is heard in a higher court. Although unauthorised access is usually tried in the lower courts only, where the case forms part of a charge under the ulterior intent offence, the higher courts may take action and try the accused for the unauthorised access offence alone, if the ulterior intent cannot be proved.

2.3   The Unauthorised Modification Offence

Section 3(1):

> **A person is guilty of an offence if –**
>
> > **(a)   he does any act which causes an unauthorised modification of the contents of any computer; and**
> >
> > **(b)   at the time when he does the act he has the requisite intent and the requisite knowledge.**

The 'knowledge' that the modifier has to have to be considered guilty is that he is unauthorised to carry out the change which he effects; the 'requisite intent' must be malicious. In particular, according to Section 3(2):

> ...**The requisite intent is an intent to cause a modification of the contents of any computer and by so doing** –
>
> **(a) to impair the operation of any computer;**
>
> **(b) to prevent or hinder access to any program or data held in any computer; or**
>
> **(c) to impair the operation of any such program or the reliability of any such data.**

Section 3(3) states:

> **The intent need not be directed at** –
>
> **(a) any particular computer;**
>
> **(b) any particular program or data or a program or data of any particular kind; or**
>
> **(c) any particular modification or modification of any particular kind.**

A person charged under this Section may be tried in either category of court, and, if found guilty, can face up to five years in prison and/or an unlimited fine. If a magistrate believes that a sentence in excess of six months is called for, he must pass the case up to a higher court. A person acquitted on a charge under Section 3 can still be found guilty of unauthorised access (Section 1); in such a case the verdict can be decided and sentence passed in both sorts of court.

The *unauthorised modification* offence means causing any modification of programs and data held in the computer, in the knowledge that this is unauthorised and with the deliberate intent to impair the operation of the computer. Lack of authority is demonstrated in the same way as for the unauthorised access offence, by showing that someone clearly does not have the consent of the person entitled to prevent the modification.

Anyone who changes a single bit with the intention of corrupting the data will be covered by this offence. Those who make such changes with an eye to profit may find themselves on the wrong side of both Sections 2 and 3 (Ulterior Intent and Unauthorised Modification). It will apply to anyone who extends an access control authorisation file to include a password of his own devising. It will also include anyone who deletes any authorised user's password.

Other alterations to software are also included. Persons introducing Trojan Horses, logic bombs, time bombs, viruses or other intentionally destructive items into the software will fall foul of the law. The Act, if it had been in force at the time, would have been applicable to the purveyors of the notorious AIDS diskette, which effectively prevented users from obtaining access to their own software. Viruses which are developed for the purpose of causing trouble and then released on the world of PC users are undoubtedly malicious and will constitute an offence. It does not matter that the virus producer does not know in advance which computers will be affected.

It will also be immaterial under the Act if the modification is permanent or only temporary. Provided that the intent is to impair in some way, it will not matter either if the damage is done at once, or will be done at some time in the future. In the case of a logic bomb for example, the person introducing it to the computer would have had the intent at the time he did so. The fact that the damage would not occur unless some other circumstance arose (for example, the perpetrator being dismissed from his employment) does not lessen the intent. The modification, although harmless at the time, would have already been made.

Viruses are often introduced into PCs or networks by naive users desirous of loading some computer game or other software which they have come by through some unorthodox means. In so doing they may have flouted all the organisation's procedures, but, because they meant no harm, they would not be guilty of the offence; of course, they would still be subject to internal disciplinary procedures. The law could, however, be invoked against the producers of the virus and those that knowingly distributed the virus, even though they had no direct contact with any of the computers affected.

The Act ignores the recommendations of the Scottish Law Commission (Appendix A), in that it does not apply to reckless or accidental damage.

Certain end-users will have the right to update data, so they will face no possibility of a charge, provided they restrict themselves to what they are supposed to do. A programmer employed by the organisation concerned will have authority, within certain limits, to carry out changes to software. However, he may make mistakes so that the result of the change is not what was intended by the organisation. On that basis he could be judged to have carried out an unauthorised modification but he will be saved from prosecution by his not having the 'requisite (malicious) intent'. Furthermore, this Act makes no attempt to control those authorised users who misuse their authority in order to facilitate a felony.

The *unauthorised modification* offence has been introduced to remedy the uncertainty which existed, and which still persists, concerning the application of the Criminal Damage Act 1971 to damage to computer data and programs. With the inception of the new offence it would be unfair to be able to prosecute anyone under two separate pieces of legislation for the same criminal act. For this reason, damage to data and programs alone is removed from the domain of the Criminal Damage Act by Section 3(6) of the Computer Misuse Act. If however, a modification directly results in physical damage, such as crashing the heads, The Criminal Damage Act 1971 would apply.

3   Proving the Crime

INTRODUCTION

As previously stated, the Act will provide the means to prosecute those who deliberately and without authority interfere with computer systems. The computer user will no longer need to rely on inappropriate laws, adapted to fit the computer age.

However, the miscreant must first be caught and then it must be proved that he had the intention to access or modify the computer system and that he knew that he did not have authority to do so. Those breaking in from outside will probably be unable to show that they had the necessary consent, but to prove that a member of staff intentionally exceeded his authority, it must first be shown that he had been told exactly what the limits of his authority were. This should be achieved by a combination of Procedural and Logical security (see 4.1 and 4.3). To prove intent it must be shown that the action carried out could have only been done so deliberately and that there was no possibility of the action being accidental; it is therefore necessary to show that there were physical and logical access control barriers in place (4.2 and 4.3) which could have only been surmounted by someone determined to gain access and carry out an unauthorised action.

3.1   Collection of Evidence

When investigating a suspected offence and collecting evidence which may have to withstand cross examination in a Court of Law, it is vital that the 'Rules of Evidence' are followed scrupulously. Uninformed investigation may actually lead to the impairment, destruction or inadmissability of crucial evidence.

Therefore, before embarking on any investigation precautions must be taken. For example, two full copies of the system prior to and after the event must be kept for evidential purposes, marked, sealed, kept secure and in conditions where they will not degrade, together with print-outs which can also be used to back up first hand observation.

Thus, it is essential that unless the inquiry is carried out by auditors or security officers trained in investigative procedures and interviewing techniques, the police are consulted for advice at a very early stage.

A lot of discussion was devoted, during the Committee stages of the Bill, to the question of the police being given powers to tap the lines of suspected hackers. It became clear that under the Interception of Communications Act 1985 the authorities already have such powers to tap lines if they have the permission of one of the parties. When an installation believes that it is a victim of unauthorised access it should invite the police to investigate. The police will be able to monitor the line (with the help of the telecommunications operator) with the consent of the victim.

Warrants are usually issued only in the case of indictable offences. These are offences tried by the higher courts, which, for the Computer Misuse Act, means only the ulterior intent and unauthorised modification offences. However, Section 14 of the Act extends the availability of warrants to unauthorised access offences. Warrants must be obtained from a circuit judge and will entitle a constable to enter and search premises, using necessary reasonable force, and to seize appropriate evidence.

The acceptability of computer generated evidence is governed by Section 23 of the Criminal Justice Act 1988 and Section 69 of the Police and Criminal Evidence Act 1984. The courts like to be able to cross-examine a witness, and a computer print-out or hexadecimal dump does not lend itself to this process. Any computer evidence must, therefore, be supported by a person who is willing to attest to its accuracy and be prepared to field questions.

The court will wish to be assured that the evidence being produced was part of an established and tested routine and that the computer was working correctly at the time. This contention becomes more difficult to maintain where the case is about someone misusing the computer. If the computer system was subject to interference, how can anyone be sure that any particular routine was still working correctly? It will, therefore, be necessary to show that the routines which point at the offender were not those that were corrupted by his actions.

3.2   Establishing the Offence

To prove one of the computer misuse offences the following points must be established:

For the Unauthorised Access Offence (Section 1)

- That the computer performed a function as a consequence of seeking or gaining access;
- that the access was unauthorised;
- that the person concerned knew that the access was unauthorised.

For the Ulterior Intent Offence (Section 2)

- That the computer performed a function as a consequence of seeking or gaining access;
- that the access was unauthorised;
- that the person concerned knew that the access was unauthorised;
- that the access was a preliminary to the commission or facilitation of a serious other offence.

For the Unauthorised Modification Offence (Section 3)

- That modification to computer material was, or would have been, caused;
- that the modification was unauthorised;
- that the person concerned knew that the modification was unauthorised;
- that the intention behind the modification was to impair the operation of the computer in some way.

3.2.1 Unauthorised Access

To establish that any unauthorised access has taken place it will be necessary to have an access control system with a secure log which records all significant events. The log can be used to prove that either attempted or successful access was made from a certain terminal or through a known port at a certain time. The log may also show what the function was that the unauthorised action caused; even the recording of the unauthorised action on the log will count as a function. The investigations necessary to follow up any misuse of telephone lines will have to be left to the authorities, but at least the user can explore the misuse of his own local networks and private lines.

This exploration will be largely dependent on finding out who was using a particular node or terminal at the time in question. If a password or other access control token is used, some evidence of identity can be obtained from the authorised user. Any access control system that identified a user and then let them obtain access to data beyond their authority would be woefully inadequate, so it is unlikely that the identity of an interloper can be gained directly from the token he has used. However, by questioning the rightful user of the token it should be possible to determine whether that user has shared a password or lost a physical access token or left such a token in a place where it can be borrowed.

However, should an authorised user have left his terminal logged-on and unattended it will be very much more difficult to prove that the interloper knew that what he was doing was not authorised. In this, and other cases, a statement by the authorised user, whose identity is linked with the event under investigation, to the effect that he did not access the computer system at the date and time indicated on the log, or that he did not access the systems or data recorded, will assist in establishing the fact that someone is illegally masquerading as an authorised user. Similarly, the recording of repeated unsuccessful log-on attempts using incorrect user identities or passwords will indicate an attempt to break into a computer system; all such reports should be followed up as quickly as possible, even though they may only have been caused by an authorised user who has forgotten his password.

It is, of course, very important that the date and time recorded on any log is accurate, otherwise the information they contain will be of little use.

Some of this information will be helpful in limiting the number of suspect interlopers. The strength of the access control system will determine how valuable its evidence is, but it should, if possible, be supported either by a properly obtained confession of access or by an eye witness corroboration.

Once the culprit admits or is shown to have accessed the computer in question, it must be determined whether the access was both deliberate and unauthorised and whether the perpetrator knew this. For these purposes it will be necessary to have proper physical and logical access control (see 4.2 and 4.3 below).

3.2.2   Ulterior Intent

It will be more difficult to prove the ulterior intent offence of Section 2. Assistance will be given by evidence which can show that the unauthorised access was repeated in a consistent manner; again this will require the use of an access control log. The type of ulterior intent offence may only be guessed at, possibly from the nature of the data or system accessed (eg financial, personnel), which should be followed by the search for evidence which supports the theory (eg the setting up of bank accounts). At this stage, expert help from the police or other authorities will be required.

3.2.3   Unauthorised Modification

Proof of unauthorised modification will be assisted if the time the modification occured can be established with reasonable accuracy. Frequent back-ups and prints from data or software will be of help here. The access control system should differentiate between update and retrieval, and between accesses to test and live versions of programs and data. Particular restrictions should be put in the way of reorganisation of libraries or of databases. Additionally, any updates should be logged for subsequent investigation either by the update application program in the case of data, or by the library update routine in the case of software. Of course, this will not help where the intruder by-passes the normal method of update. Again the rule must be that as many checks as possible must be made on the updates which are done and as many barriers as possible placed in the way of anyone attempting modification without authority.

It must be made clear to each member of staff what the limits set to modification of data and software are for that member. Disciplinary procedures should be invoked if staff deliberately or recklessly exceed these limits. If they do so deliberately, Section 3 can be brought into use, provided that their intention was malicious. This may be the case if they have deliberately introduced a virus, Trojan Horse or any sort of destructive or corrupting software, or if they have deliberately corrupted the data. Staff members may be able to claim that they did not know what they were doing. This claim will be difficult to sustain if they flouted all instructions and ingeniously found ways round all the barriers placed in their way. Skill in breaking through the security measures does not co-exist easily with ignorance of the harm being done.

In most cases it can be presumed that if proper physical and technical security is in operation, outsiders will not have consent to update or modify computer software or data, whether this be achieved by sending floppy disks through the post, by electronic access or by physical access where someone has left their computer unguarded. Proving malice might be more difficult, but, as with the staff, if they deliberately flout all the warnings and insist on finding ways into the system, it will be up to them to show that their intentions were not disruptive.

Some outsiders will be permitted to carry out updates. These will be people who have access to their own records, such as Prestel subscribers, or those that control records on some shared database. In these cases there will be a contract between the subscribers and the holder of the data. This must specify that each subscriber must only modify his own records and that any attempts to change others will be in breach of the contract and may bring prosecution under the Computer Misuse Act.

3.3 Jurisdiction

One of the characteristics of computer crime is that it can be committed from remote locations by using the telecommunications system. Such locations are not, of course, confined to this country. It is quite possible for the malefactor to be in one country, the relevant computer in another, and the victim in a third. This raises difficult questions of jurisdiction, since the convention is that Acts of Parliament apply only within the shores of the United Kingdom. The Act surmounts this by claiming jurisdiction whenever there is a link with any of the countries of the UK.† The link can be established by the alleged offence being carried out in the UK or any of the affected computers being in the UK.

This has implications for enforcement of the Act. It means that, in certain circumstances, where access occurs from abroad, it may be possible to bring a prosecution. Where the misuse involves a call-in over telephone lines for example, this will require co-operation between telecommunications operators in the different countries, and the respective police forces. The arrangements for co-operation between the latter have been reinforced by the Criminal Justice Act 1990, which provides for mutual co-operation in the enforcement of law.

† Note: The United Kingdom (UK) includes England, Wales, Scotland and Northern Ireland. Jurisdiction does not extend to the Channel Islands or the Isle of Man.

The eventual prosecution may depend on the extradition of a person, which will only be possible for the indictable offences, defined by Sections 2 and 3. A number of practical difficulties will need to be overcome to secure a successful prosecution where the person and the evidence need to be obtained from abroad.

Complications arise over the ulterior intent of Section 2. This requires two component parts, the unauthorised access and the further offence, such as fraud, which the unauthorised access is intended to assist. There is no difficulty when both parts of the alleged offence take place or are planned to take place within the UK. Problems arise when one of them takes effect abroad; however, assuming there is a link as described above, the jurisdiction rules enable the offences to be prosecuted. Thus, in cases where the initial hacking is done abroad but the further offence is intended within the UK, the British courts may claim jurisdiction. Conversely where the hacking is a UK activity but the further offence is planned beyond these shores, the same claim is made. However, in this case the jurisdiction also depends on two other features. First, that the conduct would constitute an offence here. Second, that it would be punishable under the law of the other country. For example, in relation to the ulterior intent offence the further offence would have to correspond to a serious offence in the UK (attracting a maximum term of imprisonment of five years or more) and be punishable under the foreign law.

If the UK courts can establish jurisdiction then, as far as Magistrates' Courts are concerned, there is the question of where the case should be heard. Similar criteria to those above apply for this purpose. The relevant court can be either the one responsible for the area where the accused was located when the unauthorised access was instigated, or the court in whose area the affected computer was situated.

In addition to being charged with the three basic offences, a person may be charged with the subsidiary offences of conspiring to commit, attempting to commit or incitement to commit any of the offences specified by this Act.

4 Preventing Computer Misuse

Unlike the Data Protection Act and the Companies Act there is no absolute requirement for any level of IT computer security to be introduced to comply with the Computer Misuse Act. However, if the security is inadequate, it may not be obvious whether any breach of confidentiality or modification has taken place; even if this is established, it may not be possible to identify the intruder. Even if identity can be proved, it will be very difficult to show that the intruder deliberately sought access where he knew he was not permitted.

Therefore, even if a successful prosecution can be brought, it is unlikely that the losses incurred through computer misuse will be fully recoverable and the prudent computer user will place as many barriers in the way of an interloper as possible.

Good security should be based upon an analysis of the actual risks which a particular organisation may face, so that those threats which pose the greatest risk are properly countered. Security can be thought of as being of three types: organisational, physical and logical.

4.1 Organisational Security

Organisational security should set standards for staff and monitor any deviation from these standards. Its aim is to encourage a commitment to IT security among authorised users of the system. This is best done by Corporate IT Security Policy (see Chapter 5), agreed at the top of the organisation and promulgated to all staff.

Change control is very important as, without it, the results of programs can be altered beyond recognition. It will be hard to identify unauthorised changes to the system if there is no recognised way of submitting authorised changes. Test versions may only be accepted as 'live' after exhaustive testing and with the approval of the end-user and, if financial systems are involved, the auditor. Changes to data format must be subject to similar restrictions while changes to individual data items must be restricted to the end-user concerned and that user's delegated staff.

While in post, staff should be subject to the 'rules of need to know', division of duties and no sole expertise. By ensuring that individuals only see what they need for their duties, that no one has control of an entire job from start to finish and that there is never only one specialist in any field, many of the opportunities for fraud or extortion will be removed. Individuals should not be placed in positions of trust until their antecedents have been checked. When staff are appointed, change roles or leave the organisation altogether, their access rights should be reviewed and always cancelled on departure. This is particularly important when employees leave under strained circumstances or are dismissed; such staff are likely to feel uncharitable towards their ex-employers. Their feelings may lead to unauthorised attempts to access the system and corrupt it.

Systems, particularly the sensitive ones, should include controls so that misuse and discrepancies show up early on. This allows for early investigation of any fault and discourages large scale fraud. Many of the incidents detected will be trivial; nevertheless they should be followed up. By investigating all errors as they appear, a computer user gains the reputation of being security conscious. That user is then less likely to attract any of the offences described in the Act.

4.2   Physical Security

Physical security covers the control of access to the computer equipment and to the premises and site in which the equipment may be found. Good physical security will protect the IT equipment from intruders and additionally give greater protection to the premises and the lives and property of the staff that work there.

The Act does not cover purely physical damage to computer equipment which is unconnected with the access or modification offences, but this is still covered by the Criminal Damage Act. Nevertheless, by restricting physical access to equipment, the chances of data and programs being misused by staff or outsiders are lessened.

People outside the organisation cannot be expected to read the internal regulations. In most cases they may be supposed to assume that they have no authority to access. Nevertheless, hurdles must be placed in their way, which will indicate to them that they are proceeding without authority. Physical barriers can prevent access to nodes and terminals within the computer-using organisation's premises. If these are supported by notices forbidding admittance except to authorised personnel, interlopers passing them will be plainly contravening instructions.

Access to the computer room itself should be controlled by some automatic device, such as a keypad or card lock, supported by the vigilance of the staff. Control of access to personal computers, due to their widespread use, depends almost entirely on the vigilance of the users.

Much of the security precautions taken will be ineffective unless good versions of the data and software can be located without delay. To this end, it is important that frequent back-up copies are taken according to a fixed schedule. The back-up copies must be housed in secure, fireproof storage and at least some copies must be kept at a remote site away from the computer. Those wishing to cause damage to the data or programs will wish to corrupt all copies; to prevent this it is most important that remotely held copies are subject to the same or greater restrictions on access as those held at the 'home site'. The requirements of backup are often ignored where personal computers are concerned but the information on the small computers may be as valuable as that on the mainframes and the same standards of care should therefore, apply.

4.3   Logical Security

Logical security is chiefly concerned with the prevention of unauthorised access to IT programs and data held within a computer system. This requires that each user should be identified, the identity should be authenticated and that limits should be set to the authority which is granted to individual users. It is, therefore, important that logical security measures are taken, for the prevention of offences under this Act and their prosecution if they do occur.

The access control may depend on some combination of software and hardware packages, but it will also need some procedures incumbent on all users. For example, if passwords are used, staff should be instructed to change them at regular intervals, not to use previously used passwords again and to avoid any passwords that can easily be guessed. It is becoming recognised that passwords are not a particularly secure method of controlling access to computer systems, and authentication devices such as smartcards are increasing in usage. Passwords or other tokens should be issued on an individual rather than a collective basis, as this enables easier investigation of any incorrect usage. The level of restriction depends on whether the user wishes to read, to update or to delete the record in question as well as on the sensitivity of the data to disclosure or corruption.

Installations which do not make use of communications networks can be kept secure from outside interference relatively easily by the placing of physical barriers to the access of equipment. However, the use of networks introduces a host of additional risks. Local networks permit the application of organisational and physical security but, where wide area networks are used, everything depends on logical security. Basically, the rule is that every person using the network must be positively identified before he is allowed access to the programs or data. This requires logical barriers to be placed in the way of a potential hacker. He should be required to supply identity and confirmation before proceeding. The more times that he is asked for confirmation and the more ways that identification is required, the more difficult will it be for the intruder to claim that he was unaware that he was unauthorised. Specific details should be asked of the interloper so that he is forced to tell a deliberate lie to proceed. For example, rather than asking just for an identity, he should be asked for the identity authorised for the particular system. He will then find it more difficult to claim that he entered a correct identity and password only by coincidence. Even if he is able to guess his way round these demands, he should be given a warning that, if he proceeds further without authority, he will be in breach of the Computer Misuse Act.

There is some debate as to whether the screen should display a 'banner' at this time showing the name of the organisation. This will have the effect of confirming to authorised users that they are acting correctly but may have the further undesirable effect of whetting the interest of any hacker. The best solution is to show some coded information that will confirm to the initiated that they are on the right track but will convey nothing to the interloper. In addition any message saying 'Welcome to the XYZ system', or words to that effect, should be rigorously excluded. A welcome implies acceptance and any hacker shown such a message would have a good case for arguing that authority had been granted.

Consideration should be given to the action to be taken following a detected attempt at unauthorised access or modification, prevention of the attempt being the minimum action likely. Additionally, the person attempting the access may be asked to re-submit the password or other token, the token may be disabled, the terminal or other equipment used may be disabled or the attempt may be the subject of an immediate investigation by security staff. If the person can be clearly identified and the attempt is found to be without authority, a further decision must be made as to whether to prosecute.

A useful protection against damage caused by interference is encryption. This can be applied to programs and data held on disk and to all or selected messages as they are transmitted; where disclosure is a risk both inside the organisation and out, all data should be encrypted. Encryption may not actually prevent any offence under the Act being committed, but it can render any data unintelligible and mitigate the damage. Since the data is unintelligible to the intruder it can be used by him for only very limited purposes.

Each application should carry controls to detect any errors at an early stage. The controls may take the form of validation checks, batch totals or of section and overall totals for master and transaction files. Incorporated controls will make any unauthorised modification more difficult. If errors are detected early they can be put right before they have a chance to corrupt the whole system and, more importantly, before all the backup copies have also been changed incorrectly. The key thing with control records is that they must be checked daily.

5   IT Security Policy

The earlier chapters have dealt with the different implications of computer misuse, covering its prevention, detection, investigation and disciplinary procedures to be invoked where members of staff are involved. Ideally, all this should be part of a thorough and integrated approach to security, reflected in an IT Security Policy.

While many of the stories which abound about computer misuse (particularly fraud) may be exaggerated, there is no doubt that the threat to system security is real and that tackling the threat is a complex and difficult task. It is also an essential task because many organisations are dependent on the correct functioning of their computer systems in order to do business. Computer security is, therefore, a management problem and one which requires the attention of the policy making body in organisations. Since the Corporate IT Security Policy will be used to constrain the security requirements for particular systems, it must be approved and issued from a position of authority within the organisation to ensure it is used. In the case of a commercial company, approval of policy will clearly be a Board responsibility. In other types of organisation, the responsibility may be differently placed, but the principle will always apply.

A satisfactory Corporate IT Security Policy must cover, as a minimum, the following three topics:

(a)   Corporate IT security objectives; general IT security policy statements derived from legal requirements (in particular the Data Protection Act 1984), the Copyright Patents and Designs Act 1988, The Companies Act 1985 (if applicable), the Financial Services Act 1984 (if applicable) and the Computer Misuse Act 1990) and the business objectives of the organisation. These statements should be written in such a way that they are comprehensible to all members of the organisation, as should the justification for their existence. It should be possible for any member of the organisation to see how the procedures that he/she defines or follows and the measures taken, implement these objectives.

(b)   Responsibilities; in all organisations, accountability and authority will be delegated for day-to-day operation. The Corporate IT Security Policy must clearly specify who is in overall charge of: implementing IT security and its integration within a general corporate security policy; the various aspects of IT security (including monitoring its adherence); training and education; purchasing hardware and software; Organisational, Physical and Logical Security (Chapter 5); and who has authority to issue or withdraw permission to employees and contractors to carry out specific functions.

(c)   Corporate procedures; all organisations will have preferred ways of doing business. The Corporate IT Security Policy must state how security is to be addressed in the context of company procedures and their interrelationships. In particular, the mechanisms for drawing up and approving coherent standards and procedures to implement the Corporate IT Security Policy must be stated.

If the Corporate IT Security Policy is properly formulated, it should be a fairly static document, not changing unless, for example, the business objectives of the organisation change. This is because it deals with policy matters; an ever-changing IT Corporate Security Policy generally implies that it is too concerned with issues of day-to-day operation. (Note: Responsibilities should be defined by postion rather than by name. The name of the current post-holder need then only appear in the relevant Procedures.)

Such a policy may need to provide specific rules or guidance in relation to particular types of asset. For instance, some categorisation of information may be adopted to ensure a consistent approach to the protection of information throughout the organisation.

The intention to prevent unauthorised attempts by outsiders to access computer systems should be stated and the means of doing so (both physical and logical) should be consistent throughout the business. The issue may be more clear-cut where the alleged offender is unable to point to any consent to access a system and he has surmounted barriers designed to prevent such access.

Employees of the computer-using organisation, especially end-users with authority in some areas, may think that they are entitled to use any part of the organisation's computer systems. This belief can only be countered by the issue of a policy statement, supported by standards and procedures, laying down exactly what each end-user is permitted to access and to change, and who is authorised to give that permission. In the same way, these documents should specify the rights of the IT development staff with regard to software and data; normally they will be permitted to access and update test versions of the software and data but not the live ones. Unless these regulations are promulgated to all appropriate staff it will be very hard to prove that any access is unauthorised. Even those staff members having no need to access the computer should be warned that, if they have no need, then they have no right to do so.

It is essential, therefore, that an organisation's Corporate IT Security Policy is known and understood by all employees. Without this knowledge it is not possible to know whether any actions taken (or not taken) correctly reflect the organisational security objectives. An interactive approach, where a series of security measures are proposed and submitted to senior management to see if they are considered appropriate by comparison with an unwritten and unpromulgated policy, is inefficient and prone to misinterpretation and omission. This latter type of approach may lead to end-users deciding details of the Corporate IT Security Policy or conflicting decisions being made in different parts of an organisation.

It was stated earlier in the chapter that security is a management problem, therefore the possible consequences of not having a Corporate IT Security Policy must also be considered. As has already been emphasised, the lack of such a policy will make it more difficult to establish what is or is not considered to be an unauthorised action under the Computer Misuse Act and whether the accused could be expected to know that he was not authorised to carry out the actions he did.

In addition the absence of a formal policy may be construed to be a breach of the Eighth Principle of the Data Protection Act which states that 'Appropriate security measures shall be taken against unauthorised access to, or alteration, disclosure or destruction of personal data.'.

The responsibilities of directors to their shareholders, as laid down in Section 722 of the Companies Act, must also be borne in mind and the absence of any formal security policy could be construed to be negligence on their part if the company were to be defrauded or the accounts tampered with through computer misuse.

The future business and the general well-being of the company could well be affected if some IT disaster were to befall it, which could have been avoided had there been a formal IT Security Policy in place and relevant procedures implemented.

Appendix A
The Reports
of the Law Commissions

A.1 The Scottish Law Commission Report

In 1987 the Scottish Law Commission produced a *Report on Computer Crime,* which identified eight categories of computer misuse. These were:

1. erasure or falsification of data or programs so as to obtain a pecuniary or other advantage;

2. obtaining unauthorised access to a computer;

3. eavesdropping on a computer;

4. taking of information without physical removal;

5. unauthorised borrowing of computer disks or tapes;

6. making unauthorised use of computer time or facilities;

7. malicious or reckless corruption or erasure of data or programs;

8. denial of access to authorised users.

Of these, the following were thought to be already covered by previously existing criminal law:

− Category 1, by the law on fraud and theft. A possible difficulty with the existing law was the question of whether it is possible to deceive a machine. In many cases of fraud this question is irrelevant, since it is usually a person that is ultimately deceived and the machine merely provides a means of doing so.

- Category 7, which, in Scotland, would constitute the crime of malicious mischief or the statutory offence of vandalism.

This leaves six categories of misuse with no legal remedy. Category 6 could possibly attract prosecution under theft of electricity, but this would be somewhat contrived and is by no means sure of obtaining a conviction. The question remaining to the Commission was what other types of misuse justified specific legislation. Consideration had to be given to whether any of the categories were sufficiently widespread and sufficiently harmful to demand special enactments. Generally, the Commission, like its kindred body in England and Wales, was reluctant to bring in laws dealing solely with computers, arguing that where possible computer users should be subject to the same rights and obligations as everyone else.

However, the Commission concluded that a special case could be made against unauthorised access to computer data. Access to paper-held information is usually difficult without breaking and entering, which is already illegal. The same legal redress should apply to access to computer-held data, so Category 2 above should be declared an offence.

The Commission decided against classifying Categories 3, 4, 5, 6 and 8 as offences. Eavesdropping (3) and taking of information (4) do not depend on a computer being present, and, if they become offences where computers are involved, they should be offences in all cases. Similarly the borrowing of tapes or disks (5) should not be a crime unless borrowing in general is treated so. Permanently depriving the owner of any asset is theft and is of course illegal, but borrowing is not. It may be difficult for the defendant found in possession to show that the goods were only borrowed rather than stolen.

The unauthorised use of a computer (6) was no different in principle from the unauthorised use of a typewriter or any other piece of equipment; for that reason it should not be granted the special status of an offence. People that make such use of computer equipment are usually employees of the authorised user and so are subject to internal discipline. As far as Category 8 was concerned the Commission did not receive any evidence to suggest that it was a problem requiring further consideration.

Accordingly, the Scottish Law Commission decided that only one new offence was necessary, that of obtaining unauthorised access to a computer. The Commission was, however, anxious to distinguish simple hackers, who were assumed to be curious but not malevolent, and those who intended to use the systems accessed for their own nefarious purposes. On this basis, the Commission recommended the following:

It should be an offence for a person, without authorisation to do so, to obtain access to a program or data stored in a computer in order to inspect such data or program or to add to, alter or corrupt any such data or program for the purpose of:

(a)   obtaining an advantage for himself or another person; or

(b)   damaging another person's interests.

It should also be an offence for a person, without such authorisation, to obtain access to a program or data, and to damage another person's interests by recklessly altering, corrupting, erasing or adding to such a program or data.

A.2   The Law Commission

In 1989, the Law Commission (which deals with England and Wales) carried out their own investigation into the subject. Their findings were different from those of the Scots for two basic reasons. The two commissions started from different bases, as the law north and south of the Border is significantly diverse, and they worked in different environments, as in the intervening two years technology and 'hacking' practice had moved on.

The Law Commission appeared to hold for some time the belief that there should be no specific law for computer-held data and software.

They thought that the difference between computer-held information and other sorts was not sufficient to warrant laws aimed solely at preventing computer misuse. At this stage they invited input from the industry, particularly any evidence of computer users suffering as a result of unauthorised access.

The use of computers was increasing both in numbers and types of systems in use. The Commission indicated that real-time systems were most sensitive, particularly when their correct functioning could be a matter of life and death. The potential for mischief if such systems are meddled with is very great. The Commission quoted one case where a manufacturing process suffered unauthorised interference, with the result that an operative was nearly killed. Two other real-time systems were quoted where interference with the system led to wasted expenditure, although with these systems there was no danger to life.

These considerations prompted the Commission to think that computer-held data deserved special treatment. They were convinced by the large perceived amount of hacking that went on, its extremely serious effects in some cases and the possible damage that any unauthorised access can cause. This last point is one that causes a great deal of expenditure on the part of hacking victims. Installations that believe themselves subject to unauthorised access react in much the same way as householders that have suffered burglary. The householders are worried not only by their missing possessions but by the uncertainty about which other parts of their property have been subject to the scrutiny of the intruders. Similarly, computer users that detect a successful hacking attempt do not know how much of their systems have been accessed and whether any corruption has taken place. They will incur a great deal of expenditure in assuring themselves that any corruption to their data is corrected. This expenditure is incurred even though the data has not been altered in any way. It is not so much the actual damage that causes the expense as the fear of damage to the integrity of the system.

A further concern was expressed about amateur hackers being used as a screen for fraudsters or others with dishonest motives. It is unfortunate that hackers are generally regarded as clever, rather than destructive, and that their activities are tolerated by the public at large. Fraudsters that pretend to be nothing more than hackers or who use bulletin boards generated for the amusement of the hacking fraternity may be able to perpetrate their crime with less risk of detection.

The conclusions of the Law Commission were similar to those of their Scottish equivalent in that they believed that unauthorised access should be declared illegal. They agreed that access in pursuit of some other crime should in itself be an offence, but they did not regard the simple hacker as completely innocent. As a result they proposed two new offences, simple hacking and hacking in pursuance of some other crime, with widely differing penalties.

While erasure and falsification of data or programs (Category 1 in A.1 above) may already be covered by the Theft Acts, the Commission recommended that an additional offence should be created, that of making unauthorised access to a computer for these illegal ends. The reason for this was that the speed of a computer system can mean that any fraud is completed as soon as the culprit takes any definite step towards carrying it out. It is then too late to prevent it. The new law would mean that frauds could be stopped and prosecutions mounted before the fraud had been developed enough to be dangerous.

Unauthorised access to a computer (Category 2) would become illegal under the recommendations. No recommendation was made with regard to electronic eavesdropping (3), as passive eavesdropping would not be able to harm the data or programs held within the system. The possible harm done by hacking was one of the principal reasons for recommending legislation. No mention is made of possible offences under Categories 4, 5, 6 or 8, presumably for the same reasons as the Scottish Law Commission. A recommendation is made that malicious corruption of data or programs (7) should be an offence but reckless corruption is not addressed.

The Commission wished to delineate clearly the limits of the offence of unauthorised alteration and the offence of criminal damage. Previously it had been difficult to prove malicious damage when the only thing changed as a result has been magnetic impulses held on some medium. Although Nicholas Whiteley was found guilty of criminal damage in 1990, this case was unusual. The new offence would cover cases of this sort and the Commission accordingly recommended that the Criminal Damage Act should not.

Appendix B
Definitions

The Act provides definitions of authorisation and of computer access and modification, among others, but no definition of 'computer'. It was feared that any definition would rapidly be outdated by the march of progress. Hence it was decided to leave the interpretation of the word to the courts, which, if a definition is not provided, are expected to take the contemporary meaning of the word.

B.1   Authorisation

All the types of misuse specified in the Act depend for their definition on the alleged culprit being unauthorised. What this means is explained in Section 17(5):

Access of any kind by any person to any program or data held in a computer is unauthorised if:

(a)   he is not himself entitled to control access of the kind in question to the program or data; and

(b)   he does not have consent to access by him of the kind in question to the program or data from any person who is so entitled.

Section 17(8) repeats the definition for unauthorised modification.

These definitions neatly sidestep the issue of who decides who has authority and this remains the responsibility of the computer-using organisation. The person entitled to control access or modification will normally be the data owner (in Data Protection Act terms) which is the organisation or person who controls the use and content of the data. The power to do this is normally delegated to specific individuals. For operational systems, authority will be given to the end-user in charge of the data. For test data and the development program libraries (whether source or object code or anything in between) authority will be given to the IT manager or someone delegated by him. Of course, these people will usually pass on their authority to others working in the same field. The end-user will, for example, share his privileges with some of his subordinates. It is worth repeating that it is not an offence to exceed one's authority but only knowingly to do so. There will inevitably be cases where someone thought he had authority but this is disputed. An IT Security Policy and individual Job Descriptions will help to establish provable limits to authority and avoid such disputes.

B.2   Access and Modification

The Act also finds it necessary to interpret the terms 'to secure access' and 'to modify'. 'Securing access' means, according to Section 17(2), (3) and (4):

(a) altering or erasing a program or data;

(b) copying or moving a program or data within the storage medium or to a different one;

(c) using a program or data (using a program means executing the program or some function of the program);

(d) outputting a program or data (for a program this means outputting the instructions in any form).

Modification (Section 17(7)) means altering, erasing from or adding to any program or data.

Appendix C
Questions and Answers

1. *Why was the previous legislation not adequate?*

   Basically, the previous legislation was not intended to protect computer systems. Legislation intended for other purposes could be used, but it did not always fit the case; for example, illegal abstraction of electricity was a possible charge but, since the amount of electricity attributable to a computer intruder is so small, this charge was not likely to be taken seriously by the Courts.

   A charge of forgery was used in the case of R. v Gold and Shifreen but failed on Appeal because the information forged was of a transitory nature.

   A charge of criminal damage succeeded in the case of Nicholas Whiteley. Nevertheless, the issue of whether damage to something intangible (such as data on disks and tapes), constitutes physical damage to property, was not resolved beyond doubt.

   There were a number of charges that could be pressed into use but the results were always uncertain. The Parliamentary sponsor thought that a single, unified law would give a simple means of proving guilt in the case of hacking or unauthorised modification.

2.   *Will the Computer Misuse Act remove the threat of hacking?*

No law will ever remove the threat of crime. Murder has been condemned since the time of Cain but is still going on. What the law will do is enable a prosecution to be brought, with a reasonable chance of success, against anyone hacking into or deliberately corrupting computer data without authority.

Prevention can never be complete but the use of security counter-measures will make hacking progressively more difficult and may make it easier to identify the hacker.

3.   *Will the Act prevent eavesdropping?*

The Act does not address the subject of eavesdropping at all. A person listening into an exchange of electronic data on a public telephone line may be liable to prosecution under the Interception of Communications Act.

The Computer Misuse Act is intended to discourage people from gaining access to computers and initiating activity. Passive eavesdropping, which merely listens-in to previously existing messages, is not covered by this Act.

4.   *Will the Act help to prevent private work by employees on company computers?*

Any misuse of this sort should be covered by internal disciplinary procedures and is no different to the private use of company typewriters, stationery or photocopiers.

5.   *Will the Act help to prevent copying of software or data?*

Illegal copying of software which infringes copyright will come under the Copyright, Designs and Patents Act. Copying of other sorts if done on the computer without authority will be liable to prosecution under the Computer Misuse Act. Copying of this sort will involve causing a computer to perform a function (the copying) without authority, which will be an offence under Section 1. However, a person that took, for example, a tape away and copied it using his own computer and then returned it, would not be guilty of an offence under the Computer Misuse Act. If he failed to return the tape he could be prosecuted for theft.

6. *How is a computer defined?*

There is no definition of a computer. When the law was framed it was realised that the term 'computer' was used for all manner of electronic objects from a digital watch upwards. However, it was thought that the general usage for a machine used for storing and manipulating data was well-enough understood. The actual interpretation in each individual case was left to the Courts, in the hope that they would reflect the current understanding of the term.

There is little doubt that any form of business computer will be included in the term, whatever the size. It is understood that the interpretation will extend to peripheral devices that make up the computer system.

7. *How can guilt be established?*

(See Chapter 4.)

In each case it is necessary to show that the person concerned accessed the computer, causing it to perform some function, that the access was unauthorised, and that the person concerned knew that to be the case.

To prove an offence under Section 2, it will also be necessary to show that the person accessing the computer was doing so in order to further or assist in furthering some serious crime.

To prove an offence under Section 3, it must be established that the person concerned caused the modification of the data or software, knowingly without authority and with intention to impair in some way the operation of the computer.

These offences also create the allied offences of conspiracy, incitement and in the case of the unauthorised modification attempt. Conduct which amounted to any of these could also be prosecuted. The "Hackers Handbook" for example has been withdrawn from circulation because it could be held to be inciting computer misuse.

The Security procedures must be such as to leave anyone accessing the computer or carrying out any modification in no doubt as to whether they have authority or not. In addition a good access control system will be a help in tracing the person concerned in any illegal activity.

8 .   *Who can give authority for access or modification?*

The Computer Misuse Act does not actually state who is authorised to access or modify computer systems; it is for organisations themselves to establish this. However, the Act does say that any use is unauthorised if the person carrying out the function is unauthorised and does not have the consent of any person entitled to control access or modification.

A common-sense approach would be that whoever is entitled to control the use and the content of the data (the 'data user' in Data Protection Act terms) is an authorised user. This 'person' will take responsibility for the computer system and will usually be an individual or a representative acting for an organisation. This primary authorised person will authorise other individuals within the organisation or outside to use the computer system in appropriate ways.

The procedures should be such that each person is kept well aware of the limits of his authority to use the system.

9 .   *What are the obligations placed on the authorised computer user?*

There are no obligations placed on the authorised user by the Computer Misuse Act. The authorised user can ignore the Act if he so wishes. However, all computer users should take care that they have authority to access and update any computer system where they do carry out these functions.

The Computer Misuse Act gives the authorised user a valuable means of defending the computer system by bringing charges against those that use it incorrectly. To take best advantage of this, the user would be well advised to have appropriate security counter-measures in place.

10. *What is the relationship with the Data Protection Act?*

There is no direct relationship between the Data Protection Act, which lays obligations on data users and computer bureaux, and the Computer Misuse Act, which restricts the use of computers by outsiders and staff.

There was a move during the parliamentary process to link the two together by requiring that the authorised computer user applied the Eighth Data Protection Principle (relevant to security) to all data. This amendment did not succeed so there is now no statutory obligation within the Computer Misuse Act for adequate IT security. However, to take best advantage of the Act, it will be advisable still to deter unauthorised use and to ensure that hackers and others misusing the system are aware that they are exceeding their authority.

11. *How will the Act affect computer bureaux?*

Computer bureaux will handle their clients' data on behalf of their clients. Provided that they only access data in accordance with their clients' wishes they should not be troubled by the Computer Misuse Act. Any modification should be carried out by the clients or through their employees or agents.

Software may be supplied and maintained by the bureau, in which case the bureau will decide what access and modifications to the software are authorised.

The demarcation between what is done by the clients and what is done by the bureau should be specified in the contract.

12. *Does the Act apply only to British citizens?*

The Act does not take citizenship into account. It therefore applies to all persons within British jurisdiction. According to the Act it will apply whenever an alleged offence is conducted from or directed against the UK.

13. *Will the Act affect remote diagnosis and testing?*

The Computer Misuse Act does not seek to restrict any activity carried out on behalf of an authorised user. It does not matter if the work, whether it involves access or modification or both, is carried out on the premises of the authorised user or whether it is done within the United Kingdom. Any legal activity may be carried out by any person with the consent of an authorised user. There is no need to declare publicly in advance what these activities might be but the parties concerned should be in no doubt.